The Main Traits
of
Calvin's Theology

The Main Traits
of
Calvin's Theology

by
BELA VASADY

WIPF & STOCK · Eugene, Oregon

Wipf and Stock Publishers
199 W 8th Ave, Suite 3
Eugene, OR 97401

The Main Traits of Calvin's Theology
By Vasady, Bela
Copyright © 1951 by Vasady, Bela All rights reserved.
Softcover ISBN-13: 979-8-3852-6521-3
Hardcover ISBN-13: 979-8-3852-6522-0
eBook ISBN-13: 979-8-3852-6523-7
Publication date 10/2/2025
Previously published by William B. Eerdmans Publishing Company, 1951

This edition is a scanned facsimile of the original edition published in 1951.

PREFACE

In 1936, on the occasion of the four hundredth anniversary of the appearance of the first edition of John Calvin's <u>Institutiones</u>, the Reformed Church of Hungary undertook the publication of the text of this first edition in order to make it available not only to the ministers of the Magyar Reformed Church but also to the general public. The Rev. John Victor, Ph.D., who once had studied also in the United States, was asked to render the work of translation. Upon the request of the Church two introductory essays were published in the same volume. The first gave an excellent summary of <u>The History of the Institutes</u>. It was written by the well-known church historian, the Rt. Rev. Emeric Révész, Ph.D. It was the privilege of the writer to have contributed the second introductory essay on <u>The Theology of the Institutes</u>.

This little book published most generously by The Wm. B. Eerdmans Publishing Company is but a greatly abbreviated and partly revised rendering of the original text written in the Magyar language. As the original essay had to deal only with the theology of the <u>Institutes</u>, no reference material is used here from the other writings of Calvin. The author has projected as a task for the coming years the preparation of a much larger book entitled, <u>John Calvin, Expository Preacher and Theologian</u>. In the meantime he thought that there are in the English speaking world lovers of Calvin and his theology who would be interested to read an appraisal of his theology as it had been undertaken fifteen years ago by a theologian who had been brought up in the Reformed Church of Hungary, a Church that by God's providence happens to be the easternmost outpost of Western Protestantism on the European Continent.

I wish to express my sincere thanks to the Rev. Andrew Sebestyén, Ph.D., Pittsburgh, Pa., for his friendly assistance in translating the original manuscript, and to Dr. Carl F. H. Henry, Pasadena, Calif., and Dr. M. Eugene Osterhaven, Holland, Mich., for their helpful suggestions in the final revision of the translation.

Pasadena, Calif.
April 1, 1951

Bela Vasady

THE MAIN TRAITS of CALVIN'S THEOLOGY*

Fourteen years have gone by since the whole of the Protestant world, and particularly its Reformed branch, observed with gratitude towards God the four hundredth anniversary of the appearance in 1536 of the first edition of John Calvin's Institutiones. Eight more years will pass before we shall mark the four hundredth anniversary of the appearance of the 1559, final edition, of this great work. Wedged in between two world wars, the anniversary of fourteen years ago came at a time when, especially in the field of continental theological thinking, there was renewed interest in the final objects of Calvin's theology. It is yet to be seen whether the same interest will be observable, not only in continental, but also in American thinking; or, since today in every field we have to speak in terms of global relationships, in the Christian thinking, primarily the Protestant thinking, of the whole world. While it does not fall within the limits of our task to venture upon prophecies, we may well ponder the fact that if in the 1536-1559 period, comprising almost a quarter of a century, Calvin several times recast his Institutes, and was able to have it published in Latin and French editions, then it is befitting that in the 1936-1959 period, coming four hundred years later, we rekindle our interest in the basic motives of Calvin's theology, and in the teachings of those Institutes which already in the XVI century evoked the famed distich of the Magyar reformer and Poet, Pál Thuri:[1]

> "Praeter apostolicas post Christi tempora chartas
> Huic perperere libro saecula nulla parem."

What were the basic concerns and final objects of the ecclesiastical and theological labors of Calvin? What are the things in which we can discern the main traits of his theology? Before endeavoring to give our answer to these questions, let us conduct a brief review of the appraisals of Calvin already previously given and evaluate the conclusions suggested by these.[2]

---
* All notes appear at the end of the volume.

Appraisals of Calvin's Theology

According to Herman Bauke,[3] the appraisals of Calvin's theology may be classified as falling into three different groups. Those belonging in the first group are characterized by confessional or denominational considerations. A glance at their camp brings into view the antithesis presented in Lutheran and Reformed theological thinking. The demarcation lines of the second group follow the dictates of the principle of nationality. It is this principle which serves as a rallying point for the opposing groups of German and French theologians, while, according to Bauke, the Dutch, English and American contingents take up their positions on the French side of the fence. For the third group we have to look to the German Lutherans, some of whom hold that, in comparison with Luther, Calvin neither, as regards his religious personality, nor as a theologian, can be regarded as representing a distinct type, and should, therefore, be stamped as the "epigon of the Reformation," while others are equally emphatic in recognizing his individual worth.

As we see it, Bauke's threefold grouping, is untenable. Confessional standing furnishes no satisfactory criterion for scientific evaluation. Even less allowable is the application of the nationality principle. Particularly this is the case when the two go hand in hand, as is the case of those German Lutheran theologians who endeavor to appraise the French Calvin. According to Bauke the plain reference to "German Calvinist" is highly incongrous, as the German Reformed lack the basic factor which is instrumental in making Calvin what he really was, i. e., the formal-structural sense so characteristic of the French, the presence of which is so apparent in Calvin's whole theological thinking. It is no wonder that, soon after the appearance of Bauke's work, two eminent German appraisers of Calvin, August Lang, and E. F. K. Müller, felt compelled to lodge their emphatic protest. The same attitude could be registered on the part of Dutch, Magyar, English and American appraisers of Calvinism. Most emphatic, however, must be our disapproval should anyone make bold to suggest the slur involved in the word "epigon" with allusion to Calvin. As it can readily be seen, in the advancement of this narrow view not only one-sided confessional or national influences play an important, if not the most important, role, but, as Peter Barth[4] correctly points out, the propagation of this view is a by-product of that Kultur-Protestantismus which, identifying theology with the science of religion, has always displayed more interest in treating the reformers as mere religious personalities, reducing occasionally the part they had played to the level of professional rivalry, instead of paying more attention to that real "concern" which the reformers had undertaken to propagate. We should not lose sight of the fact that the reformers felt convinced that the cause they represented was God's cause and, consequently, in appraising their personalities and theological standing, we should not satisfy ourselves by resolving our task into the pursuit of a comparative process, but should rather strive to bring to light the extent to which each one, according to his own light, was able to serve, by his practical labors and theological attainments, the cause regarded by all of them as a "common concern" since, in reality, it was God's cause.

This rule is not directed only against those who, by virtue of their Lutheran affiliation, are laboring under one-sided, confessional influence, or in whose eyes Luther is solely a German national hero and who, in consequence, light-heartedly brand Calvin a "Luther epigon." The rule applies, with equal force, also to those French appraisers who, on the other hand, are tempted to attribute Calvin's originality to the fact that its inception springs from French racial traits and French humanism (and not from the German Reformation.) It applies, for instance, to the appraisal given in the essay of J. Pannier, treating of the formation of Calvin's thinking in which the otherwise eminent author gives voice to the opinion that Luther's influence could gain but a faint expression in Calvin, summing up his views in the following significant words:[5] "I have reached gradually the inward conviction that French influences were primarily and most decisively instrumental in determining Calvin's intellectual development." We do well if, being confronted by such "inner convictions," we remind ourselves of the fact that Calvin, instead of regarding Luther as a noble product of the German "Geist", rendered him the honor of being "God's deserving servant, and a faithful teacher of the Church," and would, for this very reason, hardly consent to being regarded as a noble product of the French "esprit." We are in full agreement with W. Niesel when he voices the following view: "The deeds of Luther were not the deeds of the German Geist, but the work of God himself, and, conversely, neither does Calvin offer thanks to the esprit of the French race for being what he was, but solely to the same God."[6]

A far better approach has been made to the correct appraisal of Calvin's theology by those who set before themselves the task of searching for the material principle decisively determining the identity of his theology. It would be worth while to give a detailed account of all of them but, because of space limitations, only the most important ones may be mentioned. All of these agree in accepting for this material principle that key-doctrine which bears the aspect of being the central doctrine in Calvin's theology, and from which all the rest of Calvin's doctrines may be deduced and which may be accepted as the fountainhead from which the origin and the whole content of Calvin's theology, as well as its dynamic growth, can fully be explained.

It is Alex. Schweizer [7] whom we first have to mention here. According to him the main object, both of Calvin and of Reformed Christianity in general, is the glory of God and its enhancement (finis objectivus, ultimus est gloria dei), while the promotion and appropriation of individual salvation is invariably relegated to a secondary position (finis subjectivus, subordinatus est salus nostra). There are others who look to Calvin's God-concept in their search for that central doctrine in which all others can be resolved. This was done, in the middle of the XIX century, by Baur[8] and, in the period between the two world wars, by Mülhaupt and Otto Ritschl. According to Mülhaupt[9] the dominant element in Calvin's doctrine of God is the "benignant will," while according to Ritschl [10] it is "righteousness" and closely linked to this the "gloria Dei." From here it takes but a step to reach those theologians in whose perception it is Calvin's predestination doctrine to which should be assigned the position of all-determining, central tenet. This mid-nineteenth century group includes, in addition, G. Frank[11] and more notably the Roman Catholic F. W. Kampschulte. [12] In direct opposition to these, Albert Ritschl[13] and his school maintain that the doctrine of predestination occupies only the position of an appendage in Calvin's scheme of redemption. According to Köstlin,[14] the retrospective inference to predestination in Calvin's thinking is not necessarily co-ordinated to the emphasis laid upon the redemption experience realized in Christ. Kattenbusch[15] and Loofs[16] also share the view that the basic factor to which Calvin's predestination doctrine owes its existence is not so much his personal faith experience as his formal deference due to the authority of the Scriptures. Representing the opposite view, E. F. K. Müller[17] emphatically asserts that belief in predestination constitutes the hidden background behind Calvin's doctrine of the appropriation of redemption, the former being in close relationship with the doctrine of the assurance of faith.

With a view to clearing up the difficulties involved in these opposing appraisals, Max Scheibe[18] devoted a monograph to Calvin's treatment of predestination, and attempted to prove that, alongside of this doctrine, the doctrines of Christ's work and of justification occupy a position of equal importance in Calvin's theology. The doctrine of double predestination is not the cornerstone in the structure of Calvin's theology but rather the coping stone. Countering Scheibe's pluralistic view, J. Bohatec[19] advanced his dualistic appraisal, according to which, in tracing the development of the Institutes, we have to distinguish between "trunk doctrine" (Stammlehre), and "central doctrine" (Zentrallehre). The trunk doctrine of Calvin's theology is the doctrine of divine providence, while its central doctrine can be found in the predestination concept. Calvin, according to Bohatec, is a "theologian of the diagonal," endeavoring, at all times, to bring harmony into the discord of opposing views. He even calls him the "theologian of unity," giving thereby ground to the unavoidable appearance that it was Calvin's object to present a closed synthesis. It follows from this that the appraisal of Calvin by Bohatec falls into the error of trying to discover an artificially constructed harmony, more specifically, a static harmony in a field in which a dynamic tension represents the dominant note. This tension is successfully brought into view by August Lang,[20] according to whom the doctrine of justification on the one hand, and of predestination on the other, call for emphatic recognition, and by Emil Doumergue,[21] in whose view a method of inherent contrarieties is evident in Calvin's system. By contrarieties he means the apparent contradictions which are unavoidable by finite man, because even the believing mind is incapable of arriving at a logically all-comprehending interpretation of God, the infinite Truth. The fact that the apparent existence of these contradictions makes inroads into the believer's consciousness is due to the circumstance that life, and more specifically Christian life also has its own logic, which compels the believer to apply, instead of "abstract logic," a "concrete living logic" to his subject matter, which "proceeds from existence toward ideas and from realities toward relationships." Accordingly, the contradictions discoverable in Calvin's system are not to be attributed to some formal dialectical process, but should rather be regarded as "proofs of that truth which is life itself." In other words, Doumergue also directs the attention to that final concern to the service of which Calvin devoted his theology. Those relegating the uniqueness of Calvin's theology to its formal structure have been incapable of grasping and comprehending the process through which this final "concern," the service of God's word, became the dominant element in Calvin's life.

It will be in place here to mention again Bauke and after him Hermann Weber. According to Bauke,[22] Calvin cannot be accused of evolving his content from philosophical rationalism, since his theology builds not on mere rational principles, nor on some speculative philosophical system, but he is rather a representative of the formal-dialectical rationalism characteristic of the French esprit. He was an expert in linking, with the aid of a formal dialectical process, different, even contradictory dogmatic elements with one another, and bringing about thereby a "complexio oppositorum." It was this formal rationalism of his which led to his formal biblicism based upon the thesis that formal respect toward the Bible is the sine qua non of all theological thinking. The recognition of the fact that Calvin's adherence to the Bible was the outgrowth of deeply rooted faith experiences, which gained its vitality and its nourishment from "the personality of a self-revealing God" speaking through the Bible, is wholly absent from Bauke's thinking.[23] Likewise it is absent from H. Weber's thinking,[24] in whose view Calvin's whole intellectual approach is characterized by "a barren process of spiritual functions." "Men addicted to formal thinking are capable of being the recipients of thought elements, without being able at the same time, to grasp the inner content (Gehalt) of these. What they are mainly concerned about is to see that these thought elements fall readily into logical patterns on hand. With such men, matters find their assigned places on a rational level, and not deeply on an inward plane." Was Calvin then a thinker addicted to such barren processes? Whoever dares write in this fashion of this theology, must be wholly unaware of, and must deem a negligible entity, the Being to whom Calvin devoted his life as well as his theology, the Being who is none else than the Word incarnate, Jesus Christ.

Besides the already mentioned Doumergue, credit must be given, for again and again calling attention to this fact, to the recent, Barth-inspired German research work on Calvin. Peter Brunner,[25] with his work entitled Vom Glauben bei Calvin, published in 1925, became the originator of a new series of books, the authors of which all emphasized the fact that only those will be able to understand and evaluate Calvin's theology, who perceive that it is a theology in which man deals with a living God; that the glory of this God is not a mere principle in a theorizing system, but the transcendent purpose and, at the same time, the sine qua non of the believing man's life, whom only those possessing the zeal of whole-hearted obedience, and the confiding hope of faith can serve, and even these only if their whole being and life had been offered up as a sacrifice to Him. In the years just preceding the outbreak of the second world war, Wilhelm Niesel,[26] pastor of Berlin-Lichterfelde, and the author of the present essay[27] had, independently of one another, arrived at the conclusion that the material and formal aspects of Calvin's theology should not artificially be separated from one another, for the very reason that the dynamic interdependence and closely knit unity of the two find their strongest support in the fact that both are subordinate components of the cause served by Calvin. "Calvin brought the formal structure of his theology into conformity with his subject matter, and adapted it to the fixed relational element of his teachings. Jesus Christ reigns supreme not only over the subject matter but also over the formal aspects of Calvin's theological thinking."[28] All the other traits of Calvin's theology can be understood only if they are conditioned on this fundamental consideration. It is our intention to emphasize five of these major traits alluded to for they merit closer attention.

Calvin's Belief-ful Pragmatism

We have to mention, in the first place, the pragmatic element in Calvin's theology or, more correctly, his belief-ful pragmatism. Naturally, in using the word pragmatism, we are not thinking of the pragmatism widely acclaimed in philosophical evaluation, such as that associated with the names of William James, Schiller and others. By no means do we want to create the impression that according to Calvin's views the value of truth is conditioned on the profit element which the individual or society may derive from it. Far from building on the acquisitive bent of the selfishly calculating or, as it is often called, the soberly thinking human mind, Calvin's pragmatism is a belief-ful pragmatism. This means two things. It means, first of all, that Calvin, through a faith which is fed by revelation strives to gain an insight into that deeply planted, immanent teleology which the Giver of revelation, God himself, integrated into the dynamic interdependence of world history and the history of mankind which, like a two-faced Janus, beholds, serves and enhances God's glory, on the one side, and man's salvation, on the other. In other words, this deeply planted, immanent teleology could be called a divinely vindicated pragmatism, since it is God, who, according to his wise foreordination is at work showing forth his eternal purpose in its two-fold aspect, as it reveals and asserts his glory and, at the same time, is active in effecting the realization of the salvation of his chosen ones. No greater task can the theologian set before himself than the one presented here, namely, to comprehend, by the aid of his faith, this eternal teleology, and to help others to understand this teleology which, as regards its origin, is transcendental, but which by virtue of God's revelation, without ceasing to be transcendent, becomes a world-immanent and history-immanent reality.

Besides this teleology of distinctly immanent character, to which Calvin is constantly referring, we must not fail to mention here also the structural, or external-methodical teleology of his theological thinking. This latter teleology naturally follows from, and is made subservient to, the former. The writing of the <u>Institutes</u> and its repeated revisions as well Calvin's whole theological activity all bear the stamp of his conviction that he had to work by no means in order to satisfy his personal vanity, or to enlarge the range of his knowledge, but solely in order that he might render some service to the Church and to the members of the Church. In the foreword of the 1559 edition of the Institutes he states in the most direct terms, what recurs also in the earlier editions as well, that the repeated re-writing of the Institutes was being done in order that it might be more "beneficial than before to the Church of God." In a spirit of grave solemnity, he appeals directly to God and to the angels that, "since he had undertaken the office of a teacher in the Church, he had no other object in view than to profit the Church by maintaining the pure doctrine of godliness."

By virtue of this, the question widely discussed in circles of Kultur-Protestantismus and American liberal-humanistic groups, whether theology can, at the same time, be both scientific and church-minded, or whether its church-mindedness excludes all claims to scientific standing, can find no room in Calvin's thinking. Notably, in Calvin's thinking theology is not merely a science of religion and, consequently, it cannot be made subservient to the standards of scientific norms advanced by rationalism. In Calvin's views, the idea of "religion" is more than a mere descriptive term, and having the character of an expressly normative concept, it embraces all that we have to look for in Holy Scriptures, and claims the allegiance of our whole being. And since both the Church and theology are commissioned to the service of the Word, the domain of theology is confined within the Church, and it can perform its services only so far as it preserves its church-mindedness, and remains wholly devoted to service in the Church. Accordingly, Calvin's theology is primarily characterized by a structural-methodical teleology dependent upon the immanent teleology of his subject, i. e., a belief-ful pragmatism. This is why he is firmly opposed to all speculative tendencies whether coming from pagan philosophy, or introduced stealthily into the life of the Church from scholastic theology. This is also why he is able to exercise moderation, and to restrain himself whenever he realizes that lengthy disputes with his adversaries and unwarranted dialectic excursions might curtail the spiritual benefit which his readers could otherwise derive. It can also be readily seen that, as the number of his disputes grew, and while striving to incorporate the conclusions reached by these into the revised editions of the Institutes, he was increasingly made conscious of the need of never losing sight of the pragmatism mapped out for him by his faith. And by subjecting the overcharged atmosphere of the theological disputes of his age to a psychological examination, we may, without a shred of partisanship, conclude that Calvin had succeeded in at least approaching the highest level possible of human attainment in that age, even at the time when the last edition of the Institutes was published. This, unquestionably, he owes to his belief-ful pragmatism.

Let us, however, review a few instances illustrative of the application of Calvin's belief-ful pragmatism in the treatment of some individual Christian doctrines.

We can discover such an instance on the very first pages of the Institutes, in the treatment of the doctrine of the knowledge of God. Calvin is wholly uninterested in such proposals as "what is God in himself (apud se)," but rather in "what He is to us (erga nos)." (I.10,2).[29] We have to arrive at the knowledge of God by observing His works, the facts of creation, providence, redemption. This is the only way to avoid speculation. When, in the treatment of the problem of creation, Calvin is confronted with the question: why did God defer the act of creation through immeasurable periods of time, he readily answers in the spirit of belief-ful pragmatism: "For the reason why God had deferred it so long, it would be neither lawful, nor expedient to inquire,... nor, indeed, could be any utility in the knowledge of that which God himself has purposely concealed" (I. 14, 1). When speaking of the angels, he calls the Spirit to witness, as He alone "teaches us invariably in a profitable manner." (I,14,3). The duty of the theologian is not to please the ear with empty sounds, but to confirm the conscience by teaching things which are true, certain and profitable." (I.14,4). For this reason, the knowledge of God is for the theologian "not merely a notion that there is such a Being, but also an acquaintance with whatever we ought to know concerning him, conducing to his glory and our benefit." (I.2,1). When striving to arrive at the knowledge of ourselves, what we have to direct our attention to is the question: "to what end we have been created" by God or, in other words, what divine teleology has been revealed in the creation of man? (II.1,3). It is only through pondering the purpose of regeneration (again teleology!) that we can come to the full realization of the depth of our sinful condition. In reality, this purpose lies in nothing else but in this, that Christ may restore us to God's image (I.15,4). It is "essential to true religion" and "highly useful to us" if we constantly strive to point out all that God has done and is doing for us, and, at the same time, we are cautious lest we encourage men to sink into slothfulness (II.2,1).

Calvin's belief-ful pragmatism is advantageously manifested in his Christology. In the treatment of Christ's threefold ministry, in the offices of prophet, high priest and king, as well as in expounding the significance of his life, his death on the cross, his resurrection, his ascension to heaven, his descension to hell, and his mediatorship, he always brings sharply out the question: "What are the benefits, He confers upon us" in all these? (II.15 and 16). "Christ was given us as a Prophet, a King and a Priest; we, however, should derive but little benefit from an acquaintance with these names if they are unaccompanied with a knowledge of their end and use" (II.15,1). The most touching parts of his Institutes are those in which Calvin writes on the benefits bestowed on the believers not only in the present but in the future life as well. From the acts of Christ's resurrection and his ascension to heaven "faith receives many advantages." "Christ's residence with his Father conduces greatly to our advantage." (II.16,16). In reality, it is a belief-ful pragmatism accentuated with an eschatological mould with which we meet in these parts. "What advantage, then, could accrue to us from being collected under the government of the heavenly King, if the benefit of it were not to extend beyond the present stage? It ought, therefore, to be known that whatever felicity is promised us in Christ, consists not in external accommodations... but that it is peculiar to the heavenly state" (II.15,4).

Let us bring in here three more examples. In the treatment of the doctrine of providence he devotes a whole chapter to answering the question: what is "the proper application of this doctrine to render it useful to us?" (I.17). He adheres to the teaching of the doctrine of predestination on the ground that God in Holy Scripture, which is "the school of the Holy Spirit," has revealed to us all which "he foresaw would concern us or conduce to our advantage." (III.21,1). And since in Holy Scripture "nothing necessary and useful to be known is omitted" and "nothing is taught which is not beneficial to know," therefore, "whatever is declared in the Scripture concerning predestination, we must be cautious not to withhold from the believers, lest we appear either to defraud them of the favor of their God, or to reprove and censure the Holy Spirit for publishing what it would be useful by any means to suppress." However, it is his exposition pertaining to the nature of the Church in which his belief-ful pragmatism is most advantageously manifested. In Calvin's conception the Church is "mother," and this very name shows "how useful and even necessary it is for us to know her" (IV.1,4). It is divine teleology which is being realized in the life of the Church for "though God could easily make his people perfect in a single moment, yet it was not his will that they should grow to mature age, but under the education of the Church" (IV.1,5). Teaching in the Church, particularly the pastoral preaching of the Word, when "a contemptible mortal, who had just emerged from the dust, addresses us in the name of God" manifests itself as "a most excellent and beneficial divine method," because it gives us renewed opportunities "to train ourselves to humility," as "he accustoms us to obey his word, though it is preached to us by men like ourselves, and sometimes even of inferior rank" (IV.3,1).

Likewise pleasing are the words in which Calvin speaks of the benefit of the Sacraments, and he does not hesitate in announcing that only Baptism and the Lord's Supper may be regarded as Sacraments because these two are the only ones of which it can be proven that "Christ instituted them for the use of the whole Church" (IV.14,20). He expounds, in like manner, the benefit of church discipline with regard to the life of the Church. And finally, his belief-ful pragmatism is voiced when he teaches that "all the articles of true doctrine are not of the same description." "Some are so necessary to be known that they ought to be universally received as fixed and indubitable principles, as the peculiar maxims of religion.... There are others which are contraverted among the churches, yet without destroying the unity of the faith" (IV.1, 12). We are forbidden, therefore, "on account of every trivial difference of sentiment, to abandon the Church, which retains the saving and pure doctrine that insures the preservation of piety, and supports the use of the sacraments instituted by our Lord," but rather "we must endeavor to correct what we disapprove" because "every member of the Church is required to exert himself for the general edification, according to the measure of his grace, provided he do it decently and in order." (Ibid.) How many schisms could have been avoided had only those favoring secession paid attention to this sober and temperate advice of Calvin's belief-ful pragmatism!

Calvin's Belief-ful Realism

For the second main trait of Calvin's theology, we have to point to his belief-ful realism, and what is closely linked to this, his belief-ful spiritualism. We could also say: his theology is both realistic and spiritualistic in its varied aspects. It is, quite naturally, very important that we pay close attention to the "belief-ful" epithet. Because here also not merely the so-called critical realism is involved in contrast with a subjective or objective idealism, regarded as a philosophical trend. It is to be noted that it was personal Truth encountered and recognized by faith, the reality value of God's Word, and the assertion of these on every single occasion, for the sake of which Calvin waged his relentless struggle.

He did not look upon his God as if he were identical with the "Absolute Ideal" and the "Purpose of the World" originating with a "Kultur-Protestantismus laboring under the one-sided influence of philosophical idealism, but rather as on the Person who, in his Word, had already sat in judgment over him and, at the same time, had mercy on him. The belief-ful realism of Calvin is nothing else but an existential response to a self-disclosing God, to his Word, and to the actual work of the Holy Spirit, and afterward the applying of the conclusions drawn from this response to the whole field of human life: in the realm of science, art, ethics, religion, civil and ecclesiastical government. It is this faith riveted in the objective reality of a self-disclosing God and his Word which makes it possible for a sinful and wretched man to arrive at the concrete knowledge of his utter impotency, his hopeless existence and the discordant nature of his inner being. What is particularly characteristic at this point, is the great, final accounting which, in sharp contrast with all sorts of conscious and unconscious self-deceptions, so superbly brings to light Calvin's sense of reality, and his unwavering consistency. One of his most characteristic declarations in reference to this point is to be found already in the introductory chapter of the <u>Institutes</u>: "Because, from our natural proneness to hypocrisy, any <u>vain</u> appearance of righteousness abundantly contents us instead of the reality; and everything within and around us being exceedingly defiled, we are delighted with what is least so, as extremely pure, while we confine our reflections within the limits of human corruption" (I.1,2). The aim of Calvin with the <u>Institutes</u> is to wage war against this "vain appearance of righteousness," and for the final victory of absolute Truth, and what follows from these, as unmasking the various false god-ideas and assisting the dissolution of the illusions originating in the self-complacency of sinful man; and doing all these by bearing witness to the providential, foreordaining and redemptive acts of a self-revealing God. At this point his belief-ful realism is greatly aided by his belief-ful pragmatism, and the two together compel him constantly never to speak of God in generalities and in the abstract, but always present him in his relationship to man, whose knowledge and dutiful recognition must always be and remain an existential matter for us. The constructive significance of this correlation with the ego evolved by modern religious psychology, is constantly asserted in Calvin's whole theology. The "Dei loquentis persona" addresses sinful man in his concrete reality and through the instrumentality of the Holy Spirit he brings every single act of his work into relation with him in order that these all become factors in man's life. This is the way in which Calvin's belief-ful realism becomes, at the same time, a belief-ful spiritualism as well.

Naturally, the colorfulness and rich diversity of Calvin's belief-ful realism becomes really apparent in the course of the evaluation of the individual doctrines. When Calvin begins his Institutes with a comparison between the two realities (God and ourselves) without paying much heed to line up various proofs in demonstrating God's existence, it is in itself a distinct symptom of his belief-ful realism. It becomes more and more manifest when he treats of the knowledge of God, particularly so when he brings the one, true God into contrast with false gods. He wages a relentless struggle against the spurious god-ideas, pointing out that the realism of faith is absent in those who are seeking a "non-existing God" (Deus qui nullus est), are worshipping the "unknown God" (Deum incognitum) (I.5,12), who put in the place of God mere "dreams," "the phantasms of their own brains" (I.5,15), and adore and worship "not God but the feigned dreams of their hearts" (I.4,1 and 3). He feels that those who "feign god," "invent god," "fabricate god," and appeal to "shadowy gods," cast a slur on his belief-ful realism. He speaks with contempt of the "hypocrites who are flying from God, yet resort to the artifices of superstition, for the sake of appearing devoted to Him." (I.4,4). The struggle against "idolatry," "nature worship," pantheism and deism; against the setting up of the ideas of "blind fortune" (Fortuna), and "fate" (Fatum) as god-substitutes; the resolute struggle against the worship of images; and the caution, pointing out that the demarcation line between the "reverence" and "worship" of images, in practical life, gets easily lost (I.11, 11); the reference already here "to the natural and expressive images which the Lord has consecrated for us in his Word," i. e., Baptism and the Lord's Supper, for which we must not substitute "images formed by human ingenuity" (I.11,13), all these necessarily follow from Calvin's belief-ful realism.

The objective guarantee of this belief-ful realism which is, at the same time, the only source of the true knowledge of God, is the revelation of God himself. The appropriation of this revelation is effected through Holy Scripture and the internal testimony of the Holy Spirit. All that Calvin says of the "mutual bond" which exists between these two, and without which the true knowledge of God (recta et vera cognito Dei) is impossible, is shining evidence of Calvin's belief-ful realism and spiritualism. Holy Scripture is a "medicine," and a "spectacle" which gives us a clear view of the true God (I.6,1). Yet all this is but of little worth "unless the way to the heart be laid open by that internal doctor, the Holy Spirit" (II.2,20). Even "Christ remains of no value to us, unless our minds are fixed on the Spirit; because we look at him as an object of cold speculation outside of us and, therefore, at a great distance from us" (III.1,3). It does not follow from this that the Holy Spirit is alone the one to whom we must pay heed. Calvin's belief-ful realism gets complemented and materially qualified by his biblical realism. This becomes strikingly manifest in the course of the discussion relating to the doctrine of the ontological Trinity. We should be warned "not to allow ourselves to investigate God anywhere but in his sacred Word, or to form ideas of him but such as are agreeable to his Word, or to speak anything concerning him but what is derived from the same Word." (I.13,21).

Calvin's belief-ful realism is also revealed to us in his anthropology and Christology. Nothing is farther from him than a vaporous idealization of man. He sees clearly the consequences brought about by sin. According to him "man is himself nothing else but concupiscence" (II.1,8). "Man is so totally overwhelmed, as with a deluge, that no part of him is free from sin" (II.1,9). "Nothing is ours but sin." (II.2,27). So nothing is farther from Calvin than trying to distinguish between a formal and a material "imago Dei" (as is done, for instance, by Emil Brunner). Calvin does not speculate about man, but emphasizes that whatever has been left in man for a vestige of the image, is but "a ruin which is confused, mutilated and defiled" (I.15,4), which makes itself apparent in the only too real aspects of "infidelity," "ambition," "pride" and "ingratitude" (II.1,4). Because "an immense mass of deformity is present in man" (I.1.1).

This man, corrupted in his whole (real) state, can be saved only by one who himself was a real man. In opposition to Marcion, to Manicheism and to Servet, Calvin emphasizes "Christ's assumption of real humanity" (II.13) and then demonstrates the reality of the two natures in two separate chapters. For the verification of Christ's real death, he sees, in the words "ex mortuis," the final proof that they express "the reality both of his death and of his resurrection" (II.16,13). As against the papists and speculators, he stresses the fact that they have only the name of Christ whereas "in reality he is not present amongst them."

Finally, we see the finest testimony of his belief-ful realism in this, that right in the christological portion, he is able to free himself and the certitude of his faith from the question: who, after all, is the author of the Apostolic Creed? Notably, according to Calvin, the only thing that matters is whether everything it contains is confirmed by decisive testimonies of Scripture. "This being ascertained, it is of no use anxiously to inquire, or to contend with anyone, respecting its author, unless it be not sufficient for anyone to have the unerring truth of the Holy Spirit, without knowing either by whose mouth it was uttered or by whose hand it was written" (II.16,19). These words of Calvin serve not only as excellent examples of his belief-ful realism but can, at the same time, be taken as a warning to all formal, and for that very reason, spurious, orthodoxy which tries by all means to base the objective reality of its faith upon the verification of authentic authorship. However, the belief-ful realism of Calvin and that of every true believer is rooted in the incarnate and the written Word, and in the work of the Holy Spirit.

This selfsame belief-ful realism characterizes Calvin's doctrine of the Church. In his view, the whole life of the Church, the differences in the ministries of the Church, the exercise of ecclesiastical authority, the power of the keys, are all bound up with the divine Word, upon which they depend, and from which they all issue. It is the Word and the Holy Spirit by which God calls out the Church and all its workers who have to be deeply conscious of the fact that "the power of the Church is not unlimited, but subject to the Word of the Lord, and as it were included in it" (IV.8,4). The belief-ful realism of Calvin becomes manifest not only in that he tries to arrive at an understanding of the Church from, and to build it wholly upon, the Word, but also as he points out that dynamic tension which, according to him, is constantly in evidence in the invisible and visible aspects of the Church. The Church is holy so far as it is daily improving and is daily advancing on the road to perfection (IV.1,17). Undesirable events are constantly occurring in the realm of the Church, but for this we should not pass judgment over the whole of the Church, but should rather be mindful of the fact that God's divine pedagogy is being revealed also in the gradual advancement of the Church's life. This is the reason why it is the duty of every member of the Church to add to his belief-ful pragmatism also a belief-ful realism.

Calvin's belief-ful realism demands of him not only that he turn to divine revelation, as to an irresistible reality, on every single day of his life, nor only that in addition he explain the life of the Church wholly and expressly from it, but, at the same time, that he subject the concrete framework of civic life to an examination and try to show the way in which God's will can be asserted within the framework of the state's functions. In the taking of this step, Calvin displayed not only his eminent juristic sense, but also, and in fact, deduced the final practical consequences of his belief-ful realism (IV.20). On account of space limitations, however, we must omit a detailed treatment of this point.

Calvin's Belief-ful Totalitarianism

In the third place, we have to expound that particularly characteristic trait of Calvin's theology which, most fittingly, should be called belief-ful totalitarianism. In the present era of secular totalitarian tendencies, we shall do well if we direct our attention, through the mirror of Calvin's theology, to the fact that the totalitarian element is a marked trait of genuine Christian faith. What we mean is that (according to Calvin, too) in all that we do, we have to make fully evident in every direction the whole dependency of the whole man and the whole world upon the whole God, and that in this total dependency man's whole existence is resolved into being "of God, through God and unto God." The law of being becomes here rule of living as well, and for this reason, bearing witness to God's glory, and raising a protesting voice in his name, inseparably binds together 'believing knowledge' and 'believing action,' dogmatics and ethics. It is by the light of this fact that we are best enabled to understand why, in Calvin's theology, faith and obedience have become twins; why he could recognize and teach with unswerving consistency, alongside of grace, the continued significance of the law; why he insists, to the last, on teaching that whatever God does is done with a view to serve his glory: this being the why and wherefore of the creation, of redemption, of election, and even of reprobation. The task of the theologian is, therefore, to bear witness to God's glory as manifested both in creation and redemption, i. e., from both the creative and the soteriological point of view. He has to win recognition for the service of God's glory, as the sole motive of ethics; introduce whatever reforms seem needed in the field of cult; and carry on a struggle within the life activities of the Church, until in the reality of the Church Triumphant God's glory will be asserted also in its eschatological aspects.

Since the apostle Paul no theologian has preached, with such consistency, the God-determinedness of man, and the duties ensuing from this, as did John Calvin. This is the field in which his often mentioned Paulinism best finds its voice. And here it is where a dynamic vitality is given to the reformer's 'life pattern' he himself being responsible for the systematic treatment of its fundamental principles. The "sola scriptura sancta," "sola gratia," "sola fide," "solus Christus," "solus Spiritus Sanctus," and the faith and life contents of the "soli Deo Gloria," as well as the assertion of all these in all their implications, are the most marked witnesses of Calvin's belief-ful totalitarianism. His already mentioned belief-ful pragmatism and belief-ful realism, as well as his presently treated belief-ful totalitarianism, are best brought into an all-comprehending unity in the words of the apostle Paul; "All things are for your sakes, that grace being multiplied through the many may cause the thanksgiving to abound into the glory of God" (II. Cor. 4:15). Because while the first part of this biblical verse makes more evident the reality of God working for man and for man's good, its second part, at the same time, by accentuating gratitude devoted to the service of God, gives voice to a belief-ful totalitarianism. Notably, excepting the knowledge of God, there is not a single field of human action in which man's whole being could be better brought into action than the one given in gratitude toward God. Serving God's glory is the most thoroughly existential act of man. This is also the meaning in which belief-ful totalitarianism achieves its finest victory in Calvin's theology. His <u>Institutes</u> represent one of the most striking revelations of gratitude toward God.

Calvin's belief-ful totalitarianism is evident already in his treatment of the doctrine of the knowledge of God and ourselves. "The perfection of a happy life," according to Calvin, "consists in the knowledge of God" (I.5,1). There is, however, a "twofold knowledge" of God. The first of these is the knowledge of the creator God, the comprehension of "general revelation." This, however, finds its voice with Calvin only as (in the words of Karl Barth) a "theoretical possibility." It could have reached the stage of reality only if "Adam had remained innocent" (I.2,1). The fact that it may find a voice even as a theoretical possibility, and that later in Christ, or, more correctly through faith, in the process of evolving knowledge of the redeeming God, it becomes a reality, is carried back by Calvin, in its entirety, to God. Man, even in his sinful state, and whether he wants it or not, is wholly dependent on God. "He lives and moves in God" (in Deo vivit et movetur). Man does not get nor gain anything from himself, because even "his very existence is nothing but subsistence in God alone" (in uno Deo subsistentia, I.1,1). Even natural religiousness is made possible only by God through the giving of "the seed of religion," and He is the one who, as if administering it drop by drop, is constantly enlarging it (I.3,1). God is the "fountain head of all good things" (I.2,1), and for this "we owe him everything," and are compelled to admit that "by the right of creation we are subjected to his authority" (I.2,2). He, on his side, manifests his glory in the punishment of the godless and the sinner, as well as in the rewarding of the righteous with eternal life (I.2,2). The very reason why God does not allow our natural religious endowment, which, as a last remnant of our divine origin, is witnessing in us of God, to be totally destroyed in us is that it may remind man, even while he is defiling it, of the fact that he is "without excuse." The sinful state of man, on the other hand, becomes apparent in this, that already in his knowledge of God "he does not rise above himself," but "judges God according to his carnal stupidity" and although "he is constrained to acknowledge the existence of God, yet he robs him of his glory by detracting from his power" (I.4,2). For this reason, man is unable to arrive at the true knowledge of God purely by virtue of his intellect. So "it remains for God to give a revelation concerning himself from heaven" (I.5,13). True knowledge of God is one of the greatest blessings (beneficium) which God bestows upon us, because "only those have any apprehension of the mysteries of God to whom it was given" (I.7,5). Just to what extent this "bestowal" is God's work, is strikingly brought out by Calvin in the course of the treatment of the efficacy of the sacraments. He points out the similarity as well as the dissimilarity existing between the possibility and the actualization of seeing and hearing, and the faith-conceiving, preserving, nurturing and strengthening work of the Holy Spirit. He points out, first, that seeing is brought about not only by light, but also by the light-receiving sense waves of the eyes and, likewise, hearing is the product both of sound action and the sound perceiving ability of the ears. Then he goes on saying: "What the visive faculty is in our eyes towards our beholding the light, and the faculty of hearing is in our ears towards our perception of sound, such is the work of the Holy Spirit in our hearts for the formation, support, preservation, and establishment of our faith" (IV.14,9). Yet he does not stop at drawing this parallel but, for the very reason of more fully asserting his belief-ful totalitarianism and belief-ful spiritualism, he also points out the difference between the two: "There is only this difference that our eyes and ears are naturally (naturaliter!) endued with the faculties of seeing and hearing, but Christ accomplishes this in our hearts by special and prenatural grace" (praeter naturae modum speciali gratia, Ibid). This striking pronouncement of Calvin, asserting his belief-ful totalitarianism, renders a firm vantage point in the face of such views as would be daring enough to search for traces of natural theology in him or even assume the presence of such in his theology.

However, belief-ful totalitarianism is the hothouse not only of the true knowledge of God, but that of the true knowledge of ourselves as well. Because we can arrive at a true and real knowledge of ourselves only when we begin to hate ourselves, and become dissatisfied with ourselves. This, however, will not be accomplished as long as we compare ourselves only with men. But as soon as we compare ourselves with God, a "fresh ardor" awakens in us for a true knowledge of God and of ourselves. This ardor is accompanied in us also by a desire to be the possessors of a "new mind." What we need, therefore, is a complete renewal by the Spirit. "A new birth of the soul requires not only a partial correction but the entire renewal of the whole being." (Anima non renascitur, si corrigatur aliqua eius portio, sed ubi tota renovatur. II.3,1). Therefore, a self-knowledge which is pure and adapted to prompt us to full humility is possible only "in Christ" through the Holy Spirit (II.6,4: III.1,1).

Calvin's belief-ful totalitarianism is revealed in the treatment of the doctrine of the Holy Trinity in his insistence on the full justification of the eternal existence of the Word and the Spirit, as a prerequisite to the recognition of the equality of the divine persons. Furthermore, as he particularly emphasizes the self-existent deity of the Son, and lays special stress on the all-sustaining, vivifying, nurturing, justifying and sanctifying power as well as on the personal efficacy of the Holy Spirit, in order that he may lay the strongest claim to the all-determining totality of the godhead. In his Christology, following the treatment of Christ's life and work, the "solus Christus" principle of belief-ful totalitarianism is voiced in the following terse words: "Salvation, in its entirety, resides in Christ" (II.16,1). "We must fix our eyes and hearts on Christ alone, since it is by him only that we really obtain the non-imputation of sins" (II.16,3). He earnestly warns us against violating the totality of Christ's demand: "Since we see that the whole of our salvation, and all the branches of it (tota salutis nostra summa ac singulae partes) are comprehended in Christ, we must be cautious not to alienate from him the last possible portion of it" (II.16,19).

For further striking instances of Calvin's belief-ful totalitarianism, we may note that he dares discuss the true benefit of the law only in its relation to grace. The final aim of God's pedagogy (finis eruditionis) through the office of the law is "that men leaving their foolish opinion of their own strength, may know that they stand and are supported only by the power of God (sola Dei manu stare et consistere), that being naked and destitute, they may resort for assistance to his mercy, recline themselves wholly upon it (se toti in hanc reclinent), hide themselves entirely in it, and embrace it alone for righteousness and merits, since it is offered in Christ to all who, with true faith, implore it and expect it" (II.7,8).

In the treatment of faith and obedience, he subjects the "sola fide" principle to the "soli Deo gloria" principle: Faith is the gift of God, we are told on the one side, but this faith must be made concrete in our obedience to God, we are warned on the other. The fact of our being totally bound up with God, and the duties issuing from this, and directed expressly toward God, present an inseparable unity here. The same is being repeated in the treatment of justification and sanctification. The key to the understanding of the mutual relationship between the two is also to be found in Calvin's belief-ful totalitarianism. Calvin speaks of a "duplex gratia" which simultaneously as it declares the sinner justified for the merit of Christ, makes also provision for his sanctification (III.11,1, and 16, 1). The total dependence of man in the process of justification and sanctification on God, finds expression in this two-fold grace. It takes but a step from here, and we arrive at Calvin's doctrine of providence and predestination. It is in the treatment of these where his belief-ful totalitarianism reaches its climax. In the treatment of both of these doctrines he is warring against the "absoluta potestas" of the later scholastics. Providence is the unchangeable law of the divine will, which, while being the supreme cause of all things, should never be made identical with that "absoluta voluntas" of which the Sophists are babbling, while they separate God's justice (justitia) from his omnipotence (potestas), (I.17,2). In discussing the reduction of predestination to the unconditional divine will, he says: "Yet we espouse not the notion of the Romish theologians concerning the absolute and arbitrary power of God, which, on account of its profaneness, deserves our detestation. We represent not God as lawless, who is a law to himself." He is above all the law of all laws (legum omnium lex est, III.23,2). Divine providence and predestination are not, therefore, the products of an absolute will and power having no identity and void of moral attributes, but are rooted in the secret counsel of a God of sovereign justice and grace. And Calvin already in his doctrine on providence declares that God asserts his power not only in the elect who are under the influence of the Holy Spirit, but he also exalts the compliance of the reprobate (I.18,2).

Naturally this concept gains full recognition only in the treatment of predestination. "We shall never be fully convinced as we ought to be, that our salvation flows from the fountain of God's mercy, till we are acquainted with his eternal election" (III.21,1). The object of our election is the glorification of the divine grace, while in reprobation that of divine justice. The cause of both is to be found in the divine will (III.21,6,7; 22,11). Reprobation is, indeed, an awful decree (decretum horrible), but its rejection would involve one in a reckless and injudicious quarrel with God (III.23,7). It is, therefore, Calvin's belief-ful totalitarianism which demands the teaching of the double predestination. It is more agreeable to God's omnipotent goodness, he teaches with Augustine, to produce good even from the evil ensuing from the fall of the first man, than not to permit evil at all (III.23,7). The reason why Holy Scripture, according to Calvin, teaches predestination is to compel us fully to recognize the validity of belief-ful totalitarianism: "For the design of what it contains respecting predestination is not that, being excited to presumption, we may attempt, with nefarious temerity, to scrutinize the inaccessible secrets of God, but rather that, being humbled and dejected, we may learn to tremble at his justice and admire his mercy" (III.23,12).

A few more words will be in place here as to the assertion of

Calvin's belief-ful totalitarianism in his teaching of the state. According to Calvin, all civic authorities can be judged only in their relationship to God. They receive their commission from God, and the recognition of this fact ought to prompt them to be faithful in discharging their duties toward God. It is the duty of the subject to respect those in authority, as in respecting them he renders respect toward God. Submission on the part of the subject to the will of the authorities is required by Calvin even when these subjects are not or cannot be satisfied with their rule, for the very reason that "even a man of the worst character and most undeserving of honor, if he holds the sovereign power, really possesses that eminent and divine authority which the Lord has given by his word to the ministers of his justice and judgment" (IV.20,23). The rule of such unjust and violent authorities is manifestly set up by God in retribution for the people's sins. It is, however, to be confidently expected that God, in his wonderful goodness and power, will find the means of putting an end to the oppressive rule of such men. As soon, however, as they command us to do things which are contrary to God's will when, therefore, obedience to their orders is inimical to obedience to God's will, we have to deny the respect and obedience demanded by them, and disregard the dignity which is otherwise vested in the authorities. Because "God is the King of kings" (Deus est rex regum), and we owe allegiance first to him, and only so far to earthly rulers as our obedience to them can be rendered "in God." The key text to Calvin's doctrine on the state can, therefore, be found in these words: "We ought to obey God rather than man" (Acts.5:2). Belief-ful totalitarianism is as sharply opposed to a totalitarian state as water is opposed to fire. At the same time it is the only firm foundation for every healthy form of the state. Forms of government and concepts of the state, as well as the enactment of laws may occasionally be subjected to changes, yet all of them must have the same end in view: Devotion to God's fear and the triumphant assertion of a belief-ful totalitarianism.

Calvin's Belief-ful Agnosticism and Belief-ful Antinomism

The fourth and fifth major traits of Calvin's theology call for a joint treatment, since they are closely related to one another or, more correctly, the latter one follows from the former. We may call these two traits, relating to the agnostic and antinomistic elements of his theology, his belief-ful agnosticism and his belief-ful antinomism.

When talking of Calvin's belief-ful agnosticism, we have to hasten to state that it is not identical with the trend termed as agnosticism in the history of philosophy. There is a marked difference between the "unknowable" of Herbert Spencer and the "hidden God" (deus absconditus) of the reformers. It is the natural human mind of which Herbert Spencer states that the Absolutum shall for ever remain unrecognizable by it, while what the reformers teach is the incomprehensibility of the infinite and eternal God who not only reveals but, at the same time, also hides himself (Deus revelatus and absconditus) from finite and transitory human mind. Even the believer cannot lay claim to a complete knowledge of God, because the possibility of "seeing face to face" has not been given to him in the span of his earthly existence. Belief-ful agnosticism means the recognition of this fact. It, therefore, presupposes and includes in itself the "gnosis" of faith, since all our knowledge regarding the revealed God is compressed for us in the "gnosis" of faith, to which is added the belief-ful recognition of the "Deus absconditus," i. e., the humble admission of the fact that even the believing human mind is unable fully to comprehend God. What is finite, is unable to grasp the infinite (finitum non est capax infiniti).

We see in Calvin the systematic theologian who stands alone among the reformers in carrying through the whole of his Institutes this belief-ful agnosticism with an unswerving consistency. He never fails to emphasize that modesty and humility are fundamental requirements of faith and, for this very reason, he wages a relentless war against man's spiritual lasciviousness (lascivia), audacity (audacia), curiosity (curiositas)· and ingratitude (ingratitudo), by which he disgraces the glory of that God who, as regards salvation, gave him the proper measure of revelation but, at the same time, hid his person from him. Therefore, "it is unreasonable that man should scrutinize with impunity those things which the Lord has determined to be hidden in himself; and investigate, even from eternity, that sublimity of wisdom which God would have us to adore and not comprehend, to promote our admiration of his glory" (III.21,1). This moderation as manifested in belief-ful agnosticism is, therefore, a criterion of the trueness of faith and gratitude. Fundamentally, the greatest wisdom consists in the humble recognition of that ignorance in which the believer acknowledges his finiteness as well as sinfulness. Without confessing the "fidelis ignorantia" and that "docta ignorantia" accompanying it, faith cannot be faith, and the theologian cannot be true theologian. While it is true that God's Word has its manifold answer to the intricate complexity presented by the world and by life, which the true theologian can implant into the consciousness of his age, yet beyond this glorious background there lies hidden the mysterious and visible unity of the divine Word, the full manifestation of which, however, even for the theologian is preserved for the day of final consummation. This is why Calvin's whole theological thinking is determined by an expressly eschatological attitude and the dynamic character of a theological pilgrimage. This is why not a single vestige of self-complacency nor any boast of self-sufficiency can be found in him. Calvin's belief-ful agnosticism is amply sufficient to dispel any assumption or accusations of a formal or material rationalism.

Calvin's belief-ful agnosticism finds its inevitable concomitant, and at the same time its own justification in his belief-ful antinomism. This "antinomism" naturally has nothing to do with the antinomistic dispute which, as a result of the one-sided interpretation of Luther's reforming activities, originated during his lifetime. In the then so-called antinomistic dispute the main problem was the clarification of the relationship between the law and the gospel. The word "antinomism" as used by us should be taken in the epistemological or logical meaning of "antinomy." Epistemologically by the term "antinomy" two laws (nomoi) or two lines of thought are meant, both of which, either seemingly or in reality represent equally valid truths. Kant, in his Critique of Pure Reason meant under antinomy a self-contradictory impasse of the human mind. In theological thinking, the term involves two seemingly opposing, yet unavoidably coexisting religious lines of thought.

Calvin's theological thinking was full of such antinomies, paradoxes, but they do not disturb its dynamic unity. How is this possible? It is possible because in Calvin's case we are not confronted by antinomies brought about and formulated by the natural mind in a formal-dialectical way, as in the case of Kant, but his theology represents a belief-ful antinomism which means that the antinomies and paradoxes produced by him are not the mass products of whimsical or self-glorifying mental gymnastics; or, in other words, Calvin's theology is miles apart from a mere human paradoxosophy, because his paradoxical maxims point beyond themselves to the Word of God, the sole foundation of our faith. They have therefore no meaning and no significance in themselves but become indispensable at once as soon as we allow them to serve as witnesses, as proofs in making the believing mind admit its own finite and sinful nature. Belief-ful antinomism turns into a bloodless and lifeless phantasmagory in the moment we try to explain it from the viewpoint of objective or formal rationalism, but vividness and vivifying warmth are lent to it as soon as we view it as a seal of faith-experience, on the reflective level of the believer. The believing mind feels an urge to be witness to that God for whom it cannot otherwise find room in the logical system of the learning it actually possesses. For that very reason, through the very act of witnessing it confesses with bitter rejoicing its belief-ful agnosticism, and resorts to the use of paradoxes while alluding to that God who never allows himself to be debased into a mere object of learning, but remains to the last the activating subject of our faith experiences and belief-ful agnosticism. Paradoxes and antinomies simply make the theologian realize that "it is improper for us to measure the glory of God by our ability" (non convenit ut Dei gloriam metiamur ex nostra facultate, 'II. 8, 2). There is no belief-ful agnosticism, therefore, without belief-ful antinomism.

Calvin had already in the treatment of the knowledge of God emphasized that "God has purposely concealed from us" the knowledge of certain things. It follows from this that if the human mind strives to penetrate it, it cannot but fail a hundred times in the attempt. And when offering an answer to the question why does God conceal himself in a certain measure even before the eyes of the faith, his answer is: "in order to prove the modesty of our faith" (I. 14, 1). He follows the same line of thought in the treatment of self-knowledge, and the reality of sin, particularly so when the question presents itself, why did God so create Adam that he might fall if he so willed, and why did he not bestow upon him the strength of perseverance (perseverantia)? Calvin's answer is that this "remains concealed in God's mind." Our task is that "we restrain our investigations within the limits of sobriety." We have to rest satisfied in the knowledge that "God was able to educe from Adam's fall matter for his own glory" (I.15,8).

As it can readily be seen, belief-ful agnosticism is made wholly subservient to belief-ful totalitarianism. This is brought out even more forcefully when Calvin deems it necessary to emphasize the fact that we, the created beings, cannot compel God "to make man so as to be altogether incapable either of choosing or of committing any sin" (ibid). And this is also the place where humility as the symptom of belief-ful agnosticism is more extensively treated by Calvin. The foundation of true wisdom, he teaches with Chrysostom is humility. We have to subject ourselves to a thorough-going examination "in the faithful mirror of the Scriptures to be reduced to true humility," and "discard the malady of self-love and love of strife, which blinds us, and leads us to entertain too high an opinion of ourselves" (II.2,11). But since this humility never reaches fullness in us, and because mere human wisdom, as a veil, obstructs us in our view of God, so "man is incapable of understanding the mysteries of God any further than he has been illuminated by divine grace. He who attributes to himself more understanding, is so much the blinder, because he does not receive and acknowledge his blindness" (II.2,21).

In the treatment of the doctrine of the Holy Trinity, Calvin further deepens his belief-ful agnosticism. At the very beginning of the treatment of this doctrine, he reminds us of "the immensity and spirituality of the essence of God" (immensa et spiritualis essentia), in order that he may exclude all possibilities of a speculative attitude. Holy Scripture, according to him, through the immensity and spirituality of God, tends to repress the presumption of our mind and God, in order to keep us within the bounds of sobriety, speaks but rarely of his essence. The biblical anthropomorphism which speaks of God as of one having ears, eyes, hands and feet, is but the adaptation of God's majesty to the limitations of our being. In such instances he speaks to us as nurses are accustomed to speak to infants. "Wherefore, such forms of expressions do not clearly explain the nature of God, but accommodate our knowledge of him to our narrow capacity" (I.13,1).

The close relationship between Calvin's belief-ful agnosticism and his belief-ful antinomism becomes markedly apparent in his Christology. Let us point here first to his belief-ful antinomism as it emphasizes, on the one side, the accommodation of God (accommodatio Dei) to us in Jesus Christ, and, on the other hand, the full preservation and safeguarding of his transcendency (II.6,4 and 13,14). "The Son of God miraculously descended from heaven, yet in such a manner that he never left heaven" (II.13,4). And this was performed because "God in a certain ineffable manner, at the same time that he loved us, was nevertheless angry with us, till he was reconciled in Christ" (II.17,2). But since God, in order to effect a reconciliation between himself and mankind, chose this miraculous mode of descension from heaven, faith must not stumble over the antinomies which try to interpret the appearance of Christ's two natures in one person (14,2). It is the duty of the believer to be satisfied with the knowledge that the fact of incarnation, and in it the unification of the divine and human natures, has been enacted for our "benefit," because God chose this way to make the work of redemption a reality (II.12). In this manner, belief-ful antinomism finds its voice within a belief-ful pragmatism and becomes subservient to the latter as well as to the belief-ful agnosticism. How fittingly Calvin teaches: "The most merciful God, when he determined on our redemption, became himself our redeemer in the person of his only begotten Son!" (II.12,2). And "as we are informed that Christ is particularly appointed by God for the relief of miserable sinners, all who pass these bounds, are guilty of indulging in foolish curiosity (II.12,4). Such men "feel an eager desire to know something more" because they are "not content with the immutable appointment of God," and they "show themselves not to be contented with this Christ, who has been given to us as the price of our redemption" (II.12,5). According to Calvin, it is our duty to assume the utmost humility in our approach to such mysteries as the incarnation, the two natures in the one person of Christ, and he who fails to do this "proceeds with impious presumption to imagine to himself a new Christ," as he "permits himself to inquire, or wishes to know concerning Christ any more than God has predestinated in his secret decree" (II.12,5). We have to follow, therefore, the example of Paul who in Eph. 3:16 and the following verses speaks of the love of Christ which passeth all understanding, in a manner "as though he would labor to surround our minds with barriers, that whenever mention is made of Christ, they may not decline in the smallest degree from the grace of reconciliation" (II.12,5).

The redemption given in Christ is grasped by the Christian through faith. It is in the treatment of the reality of faith, where it becomes clear to us that Calvin's belief-ful agnosticism includes the gnosis of faith, is conditioned upon it and, without having this for its foundation, cannot become a reality. In Calvin's view, faith is "a steady and firm knowledge (certa firmaque cognitio), (III.2, 7). and, accordingly, "Knowledge is united with faith" (III.2,3), and faith is connected as an inseparable concomitant with doctrine" (III.2,6). At the same time, Calvin asserts explicitly that this faith never reaches completeness in us. He disapproves the "fides implicita" doctrine of the Roman Church, because submission to the formal authority of the Church leads to blind faith, but, at the same time, he deepens and re-interprets the concept of "fides implicita" when he points out that "during our pilgrimage in the world, our faith is implicit, not only because many things are hidden yet from our view, but because our knowledge of every thing is very imperfect, in consequence of the clouds of error by which we are surrounded" (III.2,4). As a consequence of this, even the believers cannot comprehend everything. "God restrains us within the limits of modesty, assigning to every one a measure of faith, that even the most learned teacher may be ready to learn" (III.2,4). We have to confess also in humility that "some portion of unbelief is always mixed with faith in every Christian" (III.2,4). This is why Calvin speaks of a "preparation for faith," of a "commencement of faith," of a "particular faith" and even of a "temporary faith" (III.2,5 and 10). The reason why faith always remains "imperfect" in us is that "it is impossible for our narrow capacity to comprehend that which is infinite" (III.2,20).

It follows from this that, in the treatment of faith, Calvin's belief-ful antinomism is also significantly revealed. According to him we can appropriate the benefits of faith only if "we exceed the capacity of our understanding, extend our views beyond all terrestrial things, and even rise above ourselves" (III.2,41). Human mind, in order to attain this new knowledge of faith, "must exceed and rise above itself." "Nor does the mind which attains it, comprehend what it perceives, but being persuaded of that which it cannot comprehend it understands more by certainty of this persuasion, than it would comprehend of any human object by the exercise of its natural capacity" (III.2,14). Calvin's belief-ful antinomism reaches its climax in the comment to which he is led in his contemplation of Heb. 11:1: "It is just as though the apostle had called (faith) the evidence of things not apparent, the vision of things not seen, the perspecuity of things obscure, the presence of things absent, the demonstration of things concealed" (III.2,41). The whole chain of paradoxes, as the one given here, can unquestionably be borne only by an intellect in which the gnosis of faith is closely linked to a belief-ful agnosticism.

Calvin's belief-ful agnosticism and antinomism, as the foregoing may aptly suggest, assert themselves most markedly in the treatment of the doctrine of providence and predestination. "All events are governed by the secret counsel of God" (I.16,2), Calvin teaches in connection with providence. "Because the order, reason, end and necessity of events are chiefly concealed in the purpose of God, and not comprehended by the mind of man, those things are in some measure fortuitous, which must certainly happen according to the divine will" (I.16,9). Confronted by the mysterious judgments of God, it is better for us to suspend our judgment than to incur the imputation of temerity and impudently insult them. (I.17,1). He states even more forcefully and aptly his belief-ful agnosticism in the treatment of the doctrine of predestination. He is not ashamed to admit with Augustine his ignorance and the limited comprehension of his faith (III.21,2 and 23,8). "Faithful ignorance is better than presumptuous knowledge" (Melior est fidelis ignorantia quam temeraria scientia III.23,5). And it may justly be said that he sums up the golden rule of belief-ful agnosticism in the following two sentences: "We should feel no reluctance to submit our understanding to the infinite wisdom of God, so far as to acquiesce in its many mysteries. To be ignorant of things which it is neither possible nor lawful to know, it is to be learned: an eagerness to know them, is a species of madness" (III.23,8).

It is also Calvin's belief-ful agnosticism which compels him to distinguish between the hidden and revealed will of God (voluntas Dei abscondita et revelata). Speaking of providence and predestination, he poses on both occasions the question: may we talk of a "duplex voluntas" in connection with God? In his answer Calvin offers, on the one hand, the solution that it is due to the frailty of our intellect that we are incapable of comprehending how something can occur against God's will when, at the same time, it does not occur without his will (I.18,3 and III.24,17), and on the other hand, he assures us that God accommodates himself in his revelation to us and to our frailty, and reveals himself not as he is in himself, but as we comprehend him (I.17,13). In other words, God himself blunts our intellect for the time being and until we shall be given to understand that he mysteriously wills that which, at present, seemingly is opposed to his will (III.24,17). Calvin's belief-ful agnosticism does not, therefore, require that we assume the presence of contradiction in the realm of God's acts and in the world of his will. God's revealed will is an object of believing "gnosis," but it cannot exist without the hidden will of God, which again must be accepted as the regulating norm of belief-ful agnosticism. And since the revealed will of God always points and refers to his hidden will, therefore, on this point, Calvin's belief-ful agnosticism reaches its apparent climax in his belief-ful antinomism.

The close relationship between the doctrines of providence and predestination is strikingly revealed in the fact that the same antinomies which are necessarily present in the thinking processes of the believer, present themselves in the treatment of both. All such reasoning, therefore, which would demand that those opposed to antinomies should, at the same time, discard the doctrines of both providence and predestination, must be accepted as correct. We are forced to mention this here as there are many who are opposed to the doctrine of predestination on the ground that its presentation is impossible without antinomies. They do accept providence, on the other hand, without being conscious of the fact that the same antinomies present themselves also in the treatment of this doctrine. It will, for instance, remain such an antinomy even for the believing intellect, what we find in the doctrinal treatment of Calvin's views on providence given as the title of the eighteenth chapter of the first book: "God uses the agency of the impious and inclines their minds to execute his judgments, yet without the least stain of his perfect purity." According to the rules of the so-called sober moral thinking whoever wants the acts of the godless, he himself also is a partaker of their sin. Faith, however, offers the other paradoxical solution: God's will includes the services rendered by the godless, yet he is not a partaker of their sin. The doctrine of providence itself cannot exist without such paradoxes: "The faithful act, if I may be allowed the expression, passively (passive agere), inasmuch as they are furnished with strength from heaven, that they may arrogate nothing at all to themselves" (II.5,11). "Our good works are just like our daily bread: we pray to God to give it to us, and yet it is called ours" (II.5,14). "He who sins necessarily, sins no less voluntarily" (II.5,1).

Yet it is the doctrine of predestination, in which Calvin's belief-ful antinomism also reaches its fulness. As regards this point, we are prompted to say that what we are confronted with here is really a cross current or amassment of antinomistic lines of thoughts. A single sentence will strikingly bring out the antinomy presented already in the doctrine on providence: "Man falls according to the appointment of Divine Providence, but he falls by his own fault" (Cadit homo Dei providentia sic ordinante, sed suo vitio cadit." (III.23,8). But antinomy is being voiced in Calvin's whole line of thoughts as he strives to bring near to us the meaning of double predestination and its divine vindication. When discussing man's election to salvation it is not man's merit in what he seeks and finds its reason and substance but in the secret counsel of God. However, it is man in whom the reason and substance of reprobation is to be found and located (III.23,8). "Let us rather contemplate the evident cause (evidentem causam) of condemnation which is nearer to us in the corrupt nature of mankind, than search after a hidden (abscondita) and altogether incomprehensible one in the predestination of God" (ibid). "They act preposterously, who, in seeking for the origin of their condemnation, direct their views to the secret recesses of the divine counsel, and overlook the corruption of nature, which is its real source" (III.23,9).

A twofold argumentation and a self-contradictory duality of reasoning are presented here which can be sustained only by the faith of the elect, i. e. by a believing mind which cannot tear itself away from faith-experience. And what is more, Calvin still augments the already given antinomies: the preaching of the gospel and the assertion of the knowledge of predestination are equally necessary (III.23,13). "The destined destruction of the reprobate is procured by themselves" (III.24, the title of the chapter). Only that man can draw near to God who had been elected by him (III.24, 16 and 17). God speaks also to the unbelievers but they are made only dumber by his word, denser by his light and more diseased by his medicine (III.24,13). It is little wonder, indeed, that the unbelieving mind finds a stumbling block in these chapters of Calvin's work, and brands his whole reasoning a paradoxosophy and an anarchy of antinomisms. However, the believing mind full well knows that all this is but the outcome of the fact that "God is greater than our heart," and he only is the one "who knoweth all things" and, for ourselves, the paradoxes, if indeed they are rooted in the life of faith are but barriers of human curiosity which while, on the one hand, prove the total bankruptcy and impotence of our minds, point, on the other side, to that mysterious divine wisdom which does not allow us to measure him on the scale of our human understanding.

We can make Calvin's belief-ful agnosticism and antinomism manifest in the light of two more doctrines. One of these is Calvin's eschatology, and the other his doctrine of the Lord's Supper. There is a separate chapter in the Institutes bearing the title "De meditatione futurae vitae" which is followed by a treatment of "The right use of the present life and its supports." The close proximity of these two chapters is strikingly significant as respects the whole theology of Calvin. Notably, on the one hand, Calvin's theological ethics embraces all the relationships of the present life, and, at the same time, it is markedly eschatological. This twofold attitude of Calvin can be most fittingly characterized as a paradox unity of the opposing states of "waiting" and "eager striving." A separate chapter, bearing the title "The final resurrection" (De resurrectione ultima) is devoted to the treatment of the day of full redemption, and the consummation of the resurrection. The very position given to this chapter has a marked bearing on Calvin's theology. As can be noted, in the preceding chapter he casts a retrospective glance at the fact of the mysterious divine election, while here he looks forward (anticipates) to the consummation of the final acts. It is even more significant that following this chapter, treating of the resurrection and markedly eschatological in its character, we find next the fourth book which again directs our attention to the present life, as it discusses those assisting means, through the instrumentality of which Christ makes us already here on earth the members of his Church, the communion of his people. So the embracing of the future life, and a lively interest in the affairs (ecclesiastical, civic, etc.) of the present may well co-exist in full harmony. The relationship between the two can be understood solely from Calvin's belief-ful antinomism, which again and again found its resolution in his personal Christian life.

Lack of space prevents us in entering into a more detailed treatment of these matters, and we must satisfy ourselves by making, in what follows, a brief allusion to Calvin's doctrine on the Lord's Supper. According to Calvin, one's faith, even if unable to understand and explain the mysterious work performed by the Holy Spirit in the Lord's Supper, rejoices in witnessing to it. "Though it appears incredible for the flesh of Christ, from such an immense local distance, to reach us, so as to become our food, we should remember how much the secret power of the Holy Spirit transcends all our senses, and what folly it is to apply any measure of ours to his immensity. Let our faith receive, therefore, what our understanding (mens nostra) is not able to comprehend, that the Spirit really (vere) unites things which are separated by local distance (IV.17,10). Yet even the believing mind is unable to offer any explanation of the manner in which the heavenly mystery, through which Jesus without bodily leaving heaven, becomes one with us, is realized (IV.17,31). "If anyone inquire of me respecting the manner" — writes Calvin — "I shall not be ashamed to acknowledge, that it is a mystery too sublime for me to be able to express, or even to comprehend, and to be more explicit, I rather experience it, than understand it" (experior magis quam intelligam, IV.17,32).

Factual experience is the only, yet fully sufficing counter argument which belief-ful agnosticism can offer against that mode of thinking which is willing to accept something for a reality only if it can understand and explain it. For this very reason the believer finds no stumbling block in the antinomies presenting themselves in Calvin's doctrine of the Lord's Supper (Christ bodily is in heaven, yet faith eats his real body; the sacrament is administered by man; its administration is effected on earth, yet in a divine manner, etc.), because it full well knows that natural philosophy can in no way explain "how Christ feeds our souls with his flesh from heaven" (IV.17,24), and only faith-experience, stirred up by the Holy Spirit, and uniting man with Christ can surmount the difficulties which are presented here. And so it can continue with Calvin the just quoted sentence: "Here, therefore, without any controversy, I embrace the truth of God, on which I can safely rely" (IV. 17,32).

The Mutual Interdependence of these Five Emphases

There are two more questions that need to be answered. One deals with the relationship existing, within the framework of Calvin's theology between the five main traits treated here. The other can be formulated thus: Which one occupies the dominant position among these? We can give the most fitting answer to these two questions, if we answer them jointly, and demonstrate its correctness by reference to one of his doctrines. We find most appropriate in this respect that chapter of the Institutes which deals with prayer. Purposely no reference has been made previously to this chapter. Now, however, we choose prayer, the most central act of the Christian mode of life, on the basis of which we desire to demonstrate that the five main traits treated here, i. e. belief-ful pragmatism, belief-ful realism, belief-ful totalitarianism, belief-ful agnosticism, and belief-ful antinomism, are organically and reciprocally inter-related, and that, without any doubt, it is belief-ful totalitarianism which furnishes the dominant note.

The life of prayer according to Calvin, has four laws. He denotes each one of these as being distinctly totalitarian in character.

The first one is that we ought to rise in our praying life to a purity worthy of God's majesty. The second one is that we ought to have a real, permanent sense of our indigence, and feel our total dependence on God. The third one is that we ought to renounce all claims to any worth attributable to ourselves, giving all glory to God. Finally, the fourth one, is that in our prayer true humility ought to be linked with a certain hope of obtaining the things we are praying for. We may see a fine assertion of belief-ful realism in the emphasis with which he states that "although prayer is a familiar intercourse between God and pious men, yet reverence and modesty must be preserved, that we may not give loose to all our wishes, nor even in our desires exceed the divine permission" (IV.20,16). This "divine permission" is, however, mapped out for us in God's word, and since only faith founded on the word is the source of true prayer, "as soon as the least deviation is made from the word, there must necessarily be an immediate corruption of prayer" (IV.20,27). The assertion of belief-ful agnosticism can be found in that while discussing "Thy will be done on earth as it is in heaven," he distinguishes between God's secret will and that will of his "to which voluntary obedience corresponds" (III.20,43); and that of belief-ful antinomism in the following statement: "Though all these things, even if we never think of them, nor wish for them, nor request them, must nevertheless happen in their appointed time, yet they ought to be the objects of our wishes, and the subjects of our prayers" (ibid). — We have assigned the last place to belief-ful pragmatism for the reason that it is just in commenting on the Lord's Prayer, where Calvin, most fittingly, distinguishes between God's glory as the ultimate goal and our spiritual benefit, as the other (subordinate) goal and, what is more, he most emphatically separates the one from the other. In commenting on the Lord's Prayer, Calvin's first object is to give answer to the question, why did the Lord teach his followers to pray? His spontaneous answer is: "he has appointed (prayer) not so much for his own sake, as for ours" (III.20,3). Because "the utility" of our prayer "by which he is worshipped, returns to us" (ibid). However, he does not hesitate to warn us that the three first petitions of the Lord's Prayer are particularly devoted to God's glory: "In them we ought to attend alone to the glory of God, without any consideration of our own interest" (III.20,35). "And even if we were deprived of all hope of private benefit, yet this hallowing and the other things which pertain to the glory of God, ought still to be the objects of our desires and of our prayers," "On the other hand, when we pray that our daily bread may be given to us, although we wish for what is beneficial to us, yet here also we ought principally to aim at the glory of God, so as not even to ask it, unless it tend to his glory" (ibid). We can view here the balking of belief-ful pragmatism in the presence of all-demanding belief-ful totalitarianism. Notably, in this concept, this robust theologian wholly devoted to the service of God's glory, sets, in advance, his face against the slightest temptation of the selfishness in the life of prayer. In the same manner, the other three already discussed traits of his theology are made subservient to this belief-ful totalitarianism. Because, according to Calvin, what really makes a theologian is the fact that he always speaks "as of God," "in the sight of God," and "in Christ," and is also, when speaking, enhancing the "glory of God." The dominant note in Calvin's theology is to the last that of belief-ful totalitarianism: "Nostri non sumus," "Dei sumus." "We are not our own," "we are God's." "Towards him, therefore, as our only legitimate end, let every part of our lives be directed" (III.7,1). Never, since St. Paul has any one given voice in a more classical manner to the unconditional demands of belief-ful totalitarianism than did that humble servant of the Lord, John Calvin.

NOTES

1. Cf. B. B. Warfield, On the Literary History of Calvin's Institutes, p. VII. "Besides the Apostolic writings after the times of Christ nothing in the world is equal to this book."
2. We can not, of course, refer here to all the books appraising the theology of Calvin. Only the most characteristic monographies dealing with his main doctrines can be mentioned in our footnotes. The reader may find the best up to date bibliography in an article by John T. McNeill, Thirty Years of Calvin Study/Church History, Vol. XVII. (1948), pp. 207-240.
3. Hermann Bauke, Die Probleme der Theologie Calvins, 1922, pp. 1-13.
4. Peter Barth, Fünfundzwanzig Jahre Calvinsforschung, 1909, bis 1934. (Theologische Rundschau, 1934).
5. J. Pannier, Recherches sur la formation intellectuelle de Calvin, 1931, p. 55.
6. W. Niesel, Calvin und Luther (Reformierte Kirchenzeitung, 1931, p. 196).
7. Alexander Schweizer, Die Glaubenslehre der evangelisch-reformierten Kirche, 1847, I. pp. 40 ff., II. pp. 135 ff.
8. See Theologische Jahrbücher, Vol. XLVIII (1847).
9. Erwin Mülhaupt, Die Predigt Calvins, ihre Geschichte, ihre Form und ihre religiösen Grundgedanken, Berlin, 1931, p. XIV.
10. Otto Ritschl, Dogmengeschichte des Protestantismus, III. Göttingen, 1926, pp. 175 ff. See also Auguste Lecerf, De la nécessité d'une restauration de la dogmatique calviniste, RHPR, II. (1922). Lecerf regards the sovereignty of God as being the central doctrine in Calvin's theology. Cf. also the papers read at the First American Calvinist Conference in 1939. (The Sovereignty of God, edited by Jacob T. Hogstra, 1940).
11. G. Frank, Geschichte der Protestantischen Theologie, I. 1862, p. 81.
12. F. W. Kampschulte, J. Calvin, I-II., 1869.
13. Albert Ritschl, Geschichte des Pietismus, I. 1880, p. 134. - Studien zur christlichen Lehre von Gott. (Gesammelte Aufsatze. Neue Folge 1896, p. 94).
14. J. Köstlin, Calvins Institutio nach Form und Inhalt in ihrer geschicht lichen Entwicklung. (Theologische Studien und Kritiken, 1868, pp. 469 ff.).
15. F. Kattenbusch, J. Calvin. (Jahrbücher der Theologie, 1878, pp. 364 ff.)
16. F. Loofs, Leitfaden zum Studium der Dogmengeschichte, 1906, p. 876.
17. E. F. K. Müller, Symbolik, 1896.
18. Max Scheibe, Calvins Praedestinationslehre, 1897, pp. 91 ff. Recent books about Calvin's doctrine of predestination are Hans Otten, Calvin's theologische Anschauung von der Praedestination, München,

1938. - Lorraine Boettner, The Reformed Doctrine of Predestination, Grand Rapids, 1932. - C. Friethoff, Die Praedestinationslehre bei Thomas von Aquin und Calvin, Freiburg, 1926. - A. D. H. Polman, Predestinationsleer van Augustinus, Thomas van Aquino en Calvijn, Leyden, 1936. - Paul Jacobs, Praedestination und Verantwortlichkeit bei Calvin, Neukirchen, 1937. - The Third Calvinistic Congress had as its central theme also the doctrine of predestination.

19. J. Bohatec, Calvins Vorsehungsglaube (Calvinstudien, 1909). Cf. R. Seeberg, Lehrbuch der Dogmengeschichte, 1920, pp. 581 ff.
20. August Lang, Der Evangeliumkommentar M. Bucers, 1909. - Rechtfertigung und Heiligung nach Calvin, 1911. Cf. W. Lüttge, Calvins Rechtfertigungslehre, 1909.
21. E. Doumergue, Jean Calvin, Less hommes et les choses de son temps. And also his other writings on Calvin.
22. Bauke, ibid., pp. 11-20, 35-57. Cf. H. J. Weber, The Formal Dialectical Rationalism of Calvin, in Papers of the American Church Hist. Society, VIII (1928), pp. 19-41.
23. Cf. Bauke, ibid., pp. 35-37.
24. H. Weber, Die Theologie Calvins, ihre innere Systematik im Lichte struktur-psychologischer Forschungsmethode, 1930.
25. Peter Brunner Vom Glauben bei Calvin, 1925. Cf. also Hans Engelland Gott und Mensch bei Calvin, 1934. - Alfred Gohler, Calvins Lehre vonder Heiligung, 1934.
26. W. Niesel, Die Theologie Calvins, 1938.
27. B. Vasady, Az Institutio theologiája (The Theology of the Institutes), Budapest, 1936.
28. Ibid., the last chapter of the book. Karl Barth in his writings quite often points to the christocentric character of Calvin's theology. In his protest against any endeavor to build upon the premises of a natural theology he refers also to the theology of Calvin. - Books dealing with Calvin's Christology include Egbert Emmen. De Christologie van Calvijn, Amsterdam, 1935. - Max Dominicé, L'Humanité de Jesus d'aprés Calvin, Paris, 1933. Jean de Saussure, A l'école de Calvin, Paris, 1930. - W. Kolfhaus, Christusgemeinschaft bei Johannes Calvin 1939.
29. I. indicates the first book of the Institutes, 10 the tenth chapter and 2 the second subsection in that chapter.

www.ingramcontent.com/pod-product-compliance
Lightning Source LLC
Chambersburg PA
CBHW061517040426
42450CB00008B/1668